T0132490

The
DANCE

Dear Lana . . . Love Michael

MICHAEL CAROUBA

authorHOUSE®

AuthorHouse™
1663 Liberty Drive
Bloomington, IN 47403
www.authorhouse.com
Phone: 1 (800) 839-8640

Published by AuthorHouse 10/31/2018

ISBN: 978-1-5462-5263-4 (sc)
ISBN: 978-1-5462-5264-1 (hc)
ISBN: 978-1-5462-5262-7 (e)

Valentine's Day 1995

DEAR LANA,

Have you ever been bored at a party
Given up on romance
Thought about leaving
When an Angel asked you to dance

Well it happened to me
It was quite a surprise
Romance truly over
It had to be lies

We danced all night
Our bodies closely in tune
Hopefully this was the beginning
We would share ourselves soon

I can't explain chemistry
Or whose two hearts might fit
But I know it when I feel it
And this has to be it!

Today is set aside for lovers
And all their hearts can finance
My Valentines wish already came true
The night you asked me to Dance

Love,
Michael

Valentine's Day 1996

AMAZING YEAR

Amazing what can happen in just one year
The stock market can rise or crash due to fear
The earth completes one revolution around the sun
595 miles and her journey is done

A life is conceived and born in this time
I heard the father fainted
But mother and child
Are doing fine

How have I changed, just what has happened
I threw away some tapes, that served only to dampen
And the void I have felt since my father died
Has been filled by the Angel always at my side

Forging two indelible spirits into one
Has not always been easy, has not always been fun
But we share a passion in pursuing a dream
Of becoming an indivisible, undefeatable team

My faith in romance having been restored
A year has passed without me being bored
I've learned to understand myself as a man
And I have accepted God and His masterplan

He has told me to put my faith in Him
And to thy own self be true
Love the woman I have brought into your life
I've created her especially for you

With all these gifts to which I have been bestowed
I know now I have nothing to fear
After all, look how God has blessed me
In just one amazing year

Love,
Michael

Engagement Day 1997

JANUARY 12TH, 1997

Our fairytale began
When you asked me to dance
Having noticed you much earlier
I reveled in the chance

That night was filled with magic
As they have all been since
You my Fair Maiden
And I your Prince

Our spirits have never stopped dancing
They could never be pulled apart
The sounds they move to
Emanate from the symphonies of our heart

And now it is I who propose
As I humbly bend on knee
Can I have this Dance for the rest of our lives
Lana, will you marry me

Love,
Michael

Valentine's Day 1998

DATING YOUR WIFE

Dating your wife
For most seems out of place
But no other husband
Has seen the joy of my wife's face

Each day is Valentine's
Every night a honeymoon
It begins with a glorious sunrise
And ends with a full moon

I will never take our gift for granted
The one which God has bestowed
Even though life's journey
Is often a winding road

And as for today
It is a beginning not end
For the appreciation I have for you
My wife, my lover and my best friend

Love,
Michael

Valentine's Day 1999

CHOOSING WISELY

When you ask someone to be there
For your entire life
You think you have a good idea
That she'll make a wonderful wife

But something you'll never know
Even though much is at stake
Is what kind of mother
Your lovely wife will make

I saw the signs early
Her dedication to her health
Knowing a successful pregnancy
Is the ultimate kind of wealth

But it was the strength she showed
Bringing our son into the world
Where her colors of heroism
Were first unfurled

And every day since
In every possible way
Putting Cole first
In her unselfish way

I can hear my father's voice,
"She's a great wife and Mother all in one
Michael, you have nothing to fear
For you have chosen wisely my son."

Love,
Michael

Valentine's Day 2000

THE GAME OF LOVE

The game of love
Is a risky one
Some win and some lose
And get none

I never could have imagined
I never could have thought
Nor ever fathomed
All the love you have brought

Into my life so briefly
And into my heart so deeply
Into my thoughts so sweetly
Encompassing my soul completely

I cannot tell you the secret
The strategy is never done
The game of love is a mystery to me
But with you I know I've won

Love,
Michael

Valentine's Day 2001

THE TRADITION I HAVE STARTED

The tradition I started
While we were just dating
Is just as important now
And shows no sign of fading

Some people wonder
How a masculine guy like me
Can pour his heart open
In this annual poetry

Well take a look at my fields
And how green they have become
Warmed by your love
And the rays of the sun

To never know thirst
As the roots take hold
And the fruit of my vines
Grows big and bold

But the real joy is the harvest
One that grows more bountiful each day
With you tending the fields
Blue skies have replaced gray

And just what have we grown
That gives us such joy
Our home, marriage and love
And a very special boy

As the time grows near
And we await the elation
Of the arrival of our next child
God's newest creation

I take this time
To recognize my life is rich and full
God has given me you
And you make it all possible

Love,
Michael

Valentine's Day 2002

WHERE I STAND

You push and you pull
All the while I am kicking and screaming
But when we arrive at our destination
I always end up beaming

For you have the vision and courage
To take the first step
If I had your confidence
I would have not looked just leaped

I ponder where we have been to
The places we have seen
I know now God's plan for us
Is to live our dream

Happiness is not a destination
It is better to travel hopefully than arrive
You have reenforced these truths to me
And I have never felt more alive

I greet each day
Anticipating blue skies
Because I see Heaven each morning
As I look into my children's eyes

Thank you for being the kind of woman
That can make me a better man
I have never been more comfortable
Than today where I stand!

Love,
Michael

Valentine's Day 2003

LESSONS OF LOVE

At the start of each year
People rush to proclaim
The things they will give up
And the bad habits they will tame

For most give it their best
And they are truly sincere
But their efforts run out
A few months into the year

So I thought I would add a twist
To this annual tradition
And pledge to you Dolly
My Valentine's Day resolution

I know I can be stubborn
Vanity always lies
I am going to be a better listener
Love teaches compromise

Thinking of myself
Is a hard habit to break
I am going to put your needs first
Love teaches us to give rather than take

And I want to set the proper example
So our children can see
How women should be honored
Love teaches us this vigorously

A man's battle with his ego
Can be a lifelong fight
I will have to pray about this one
Love teaches patience is being right

Throughout this year
I pledge to feature
The lessons of love
And I promise to listen to my teacher

Love,
Michael

Valentine's Day 2004

As I Look Around Me

As I look around me
It is hard to believe
Cole rides a bike without training wheels
And Mia is going to be three

Cole's learning to read and write
He gets better line after line
Mia watches Dora the Explorer
Her Spanish is better than mine

Cole enjoys playing rough
And wearing his army gear
Mia loves to try on shoes
Just like you my Dear

In this ever changing word
That seems to spin ever faster
There seems to be one imperative
That I must master

To be grateful each day
And live like it was the last
As if I needed proof
Look at our children growing up so fast

But they are not the only sensations
That I see grow each day
I marvel at your abilities
Even though I may not say

I take for granted now
The beauty you have created in our home
I seem to have forgotten what my place looked like
When I lived on my own

You sure can juggle
All things your family demands
I know sometimes your needs are not met
And all you have is your complacent fans

Your presence in my life
Is a great example of God's love for me
I will honor Him by honoring you
And become what He wants me to be

Love,
Michael

Valentine's Day 2005

STILL HOLDING HANDS

Once is a while as you walk down the street
You will notice an older couple and
Wonder, how did they meet
Still holding hands and with a twinkle in their eyes
A bustling world around them, but
They notice only blue skies

Where do they live, where do they work and play
What happened in their lives that turned
Their hair from dark to grey
They seemed to be smiling, even as they
Walk with an uneven stride
They don't seem to mind the ravages
Of time they cannot hide

What do they know others much younger can't seem to find
Would they tell me their secret if I asked,
Do you think they would mind
It was then I noticed, each carried a book under their arm
And directly behind them was a building
That looked much like a barn

And they weren't walking alone as I first I had thought
This place they were leaving, many they had brought
It was their grown up son and daughter
Who were close behind
Instructing the third generation that they had better mind

Grandchildren began to swirl around them, busy as bees
Yelling for some attention and pulling on their sleeves
Things suddenly were clearer, as my focus became keen
I was looking past these their wrinkles,
There were lessons I should glean

That was a Bible that they carried along their trip
And that building in the distance was there place of worship
Surrounded by family and with God in their hearts
It was perfectly clear where one should start

They had no secret from which to share
Everything needed for happiness was right there
They were better together and that was enough
It sustained them when things got tough

For marriage to flourish, two people seemingly become one
That is a difficult concept to grasp, like God having a Son
It is a challenge to surrender, very hard to do
But it is the power of faith that reveals this to be true

This couple I see is amazing
To the Lord they are always praising
Their values are simple but they are a must
Do you see who this couple is now, Lana that couple is us

Sharing a future with you is the greatest joy of all!

Love,
Michael

Valentine's Day 2006

EARTHLY ANGELS

There are moments that stick out
In this journey we describe as life
Where extraordinary people appear
And deliver us from strife

We never see these remarkable people coming
And usually, we never see them leave
These messengers take our tattered hopes
Combine them with God's love and weave

They arrive in the nick of time
When our spirts are about to break
Without them we would be lost
The challenges of life we could not take

This is true in my life
There have been times I could not help myself
It was God's Earthly Angels
Who had the power to restore my spiritual health

The Lord knew I would needed extra
After all, He had given me my life
So he delivered unto me one of these angels
And he blessed me by making her my wife

Love,
Michael

Valentine's Day 2007

THE BEST IS YET TO COME

My life is best viewed in two parts
The first half is an uninspiring tale
A story full of good times and bad
Plodding along a meandering trail

I thought it was a good life
I made many friends and won many races
We said we would always be close
And now I can barely remember their faces

I had no reason to complain
I often traveled with a smile on my face
Shoulder to shoulder I was
With the other rats in the race

But this was before
My life was to take a turn
A beautiful spirit would take my hand
An Angel I would learn

Light began to shine on my new world
With you as my guide
I began to have higher aspirations
I longed to make you by bride

You led me to live in a new community
I left the only place that I knew
Starting over didn't seem so scary
Since home was being with you

You filled my house with beauty
And I wasn't used to that
You showed me the daring of a risk taker
I was used to standing pat

I took on the responsibility of fatherhood
I was confident like at a time no other
So I took on the most important job of my life
I knew you would be the greatest mother

Our children are Miracles
They are where our blessings are stored
I could not dream the feelings that I would feel
Cole and Mia are the work of the Lord

The man you see today
Is the man that you helped to create
But you make everything around you better
That is one of your greatest traits

I don't always accept your brilliance
Perhaps a habit I picked up long ago
But there is nobody I respect more in this life
You are the most amazing person I know

Thank you for loving me
I feel like we have already won
Even with this beautiful life
The best is yet to come

I Love You,
Michael

Valentine's Day 2008

DREAMS

Have you ever woken up from a dream
And realized it wasn't so
Did you close your eyes and try to return
To that place you wanted to go

It is peaceful there
And things go just as they should
One amazing feeling after another
We all would exist there if we could

Try as we might to stay in this world
Our unconscious surrenders to the light
We grumble as we leave this place
And look forward to returning later that night

But for me this year
I began to recognize
That my dreams begin to take shape
The moment I open my eyes

For 13 years now I have seen you model
That there is nothing left to spare
You live each day to the fullest
This quality makes you rare

Your lack of fear used to scare me
It seemed so naïve
Now I realize I lacked your bravery
You've given my dreams a reprieve

Your eagerness to give to others
Made me think you would have less
The quality of your friendship
Meant diving heart first into their mess

But rather than be diminished
You were enriched upon your return
It seems that giving it all away
Makes love more plentiful, I would learn

My dreams are now a reality
And for everything else you do
I'll spend the rest of my days
Seeing that your dreams come true!

Love,
Michael

Valentine's Day 2009

LADY LUCK

Having been to the city
That was built on sand
I wonder why they came here
Why did they choose this land

It is in the middle of nowhere
That they built this mirage
It is here where they fool our senses
In this larger than life fantasy lodge

People bring their riches
And then put them at risk
The odds stacked against them
After each losing hand they persist

In the throes of desperation
And hoping not to lose their last buck
They call on the Patron Saint of Las Vegas
They call her Lady Luck

But she is not there to support them
She is not to be found at all
If the Lady isn't already in your life
She will never hear your call

Why do I consider myself lucky
Why does my life get better each year
Because I bring my Lady Luck with me
Instead of looking for her there

The talents she possesses
I have but a few
But when we stand united
I have them too

When I think about where I started
And where I am with her today
When I think about where we are going
And where we will be someday

None of this would be possible
None of this could be true
If I had realized that the night I met her
That Lady Luck was you!

I Love you,
Michael

Valentine's Day 2010

STORYTELLERS

Every generation
Goes through a rough spell
That's why we like to listen
To the stories they tell

For them the times were hard
And they learned to live without
But now their lives are so rich
What is this all about

Those experiences that they lived through
And the ones we try to escape
Turn out to be essential
To the fortunes we would like to make

Fate now challenges our age
As we face extraordinary times
Those destined to fail, torn asunder
Those destined to succeed, it binds

I know the value of my loved ones
Today more than before
I see bad times aren't economic
As much as a spiritual war

We will remain true to our values
And double our efforts as well
Today is the birthplace of our stories
The ones someday we will tell

We will explain our success and riches
To another generation to come
Not to be afraid of the struggle
With us God is never done

When knocked to your knees look over
If kneeling next to you is your wife
God has given you all you need
To ensure a victorious life

Lana you are still an Angel
Good luck charm and moral compass too
We are becoming the storytellers
I can't wait to tell these stories with you!

Love,
Michael

Valentine's Day 2011

MORE THAN EVER

For all of your life
You have been the one
Caring for others
Who were on the run

Their troubles were great
Their support was low
Nothing is worse than emptiness
And the feeling you have nowhere to go

You filled those voids
With optimism and light
The people began to realize
They weren't alone in their fight

You may not have seen it
But you were leaving a trail
Which those people now follow
As you have become frail

Our community now embraces you
In a way so deep and profound
They want to be part of your miracle
When cancer is nowhere to be found

Who comes to the aid of an Angel
When she has a fight up ahead
Who does God trust with His creation
While He watches from overhead

I think the answer
Is all too clear
Your family is around you
There is nothing to fear

Your moment to struggle
Is our moment to shine
We were put in your life for a reason
It has all been divine

It is an honor to serve you
Although we could never repay
The strength you given us
Each and every day

Our rewards for our efforts
As we take on this fight
Is to enjoy our lives together
In a future both long and bright

I love you now more than ever,
Michael

Valentine's Day 2012

THE JOURNEY

The journey takes you many places
The journey shows you many faces
It chooses the route upon which you travel
Hold on tight or your life might unravel

The direction is easy to accept
When things go smooth and all things are prepped
Smiles are the result of these easy times
These are the days of easy climbs

People seem to find you
People you hardly knew
We all want to be together
While were traveling in fair weather

It's too bad the story has to change
But the emotions in life span quite a range
We tend to look for someone to blame
Because the road conditions never stay the same

It's a lonelier walk when these dark times fall
Our progress is slowed to just a crawl
Those who stand by us now
Lend a hand in pushing our plough

What is it that binds these people
With us when we're feeling feeble
Don't they see the winding road up ahead
Don't they want to choose an easier path instead

The questions that are raised
Along this up and down route
Demonstrate to us what's important
And what's life really about

The journey has been my great teacher
The misdirections are meant to overcome
The good times alone could not prepare me
For the difficulties that were to come

When the strong winds came
And my Angel was caught in a swirl
Memories of rough roads taken
Helped me save my girl

I learned to Love during those long days
I learned sacrificing was a good thing to do
You walked along beside me then
I walk beside you too!

You are my constant companion
The greatest Love I have ever known
You were my true beginning
And the greatest seed God has ever sown

I Love you, Lana!
Michael

Valentine's Day 2013

STILL

To most people
This may come as a surprise
I believe the best is yet to come
They may not think that's wise

I'm not overly optimistic
Nor am I naïve
But I have my past as an example
That is why I believe

I'm wandering around lonely
In some mediocre trance
Suddenly I'm pulled from obscurity
With an invitation to Dance

When I was hit with challenges
And I could not see a way out
When I had just about given up
Suddenly, I was shown a route

A nine month odyssey
Taxing on both body and soul
Add a terribly hard delivery
That gave us Cole

Never getting enough sleep
Beginning to see lines on our face
Ending each day exhausted
That gave us Mia Grace

Worrying about money
How could we pay our bills
One minute our account was empty
Suddenly, we had enough for thrills

When first I said I loved you
I meant I always will
When I said "in good times and bad times"
I mean that still

As you can see in our history
Losses are a prelude to a win
Miracle Miracle Miracle
Let the ministry begin!

I Love You,
Michael

Valentine's Day 2014

What Does Your Angel Look Like?

Mythical some would say
Just another reason to escape
The pressures of life
For many are too hard to take

I would argue it's a lack of faith
Our Father would not abandon
Angels help guide believers
To see them your faith you must stand on

Raphael is the angel of healing
He has strengthened our family this year
While Gabriel is God's messenger
The Lord loves us, it's clear

Awash in energy and light
This is how they are depicted
Pictured with wings and simple robes
God's eternal love they have predicted

Constantly encouraging us
They are never too busy to listen
Diligent and hard working
People's faith they do christen

Looking back on last year
I was given time to spend with my loves
My family intact and healthy
Guided by my Angel wearing pink boxing gloves

Enduring an inspiring
I don't say this enough
You're a remarkable combination
Of just the right stuff

Stronger than any other person
The fighter who would not fall
While you were receiving a miracle
You were a miracle to us all!

Happy Valentine's Day 2014,
Michael

Valentine's Day 2015

OPPOSITES ATTRACT

The journey can be difficult
And is certainly hard to master
And just when you get the hang of it
You have coffee with your pastor

Your glow is very impressive
You could not ask for anything more
You have found the person who completes you
But he has seen it all before

You mention the qualities you're in love with
They exists in this person you have found
Perfect in every dimension
Trumpets begin to sound

With our Love on full display
His warning came as a complete surprise
He said the qualities you love today
May soon bring tears to your eyes

My strength you found so exciting
Can be too hot at times to handle
You're designing skills on full display
Until there wasn't room for one more candle

Overlooking what's broken kept me sunny
Until things went from worn to bust
While your list of items kept growing
Happiness slipped right by you as you fussed

Strong willed made me attractive
But domineering made me small
Attention to detail made you productive
Compulsions lead you to hit the wall

Flying by the seat of my pants made me happy
But that led us to fall on our behinds
Your routines got us moving forward
But you missed some laughs as you closed the blinds

But something began to happen
The longer we remained a team
Those things about each other that bugged us
Began to make us beam

I like watching you get the mail
And opening it in your car
You enjoy watching me start a project
Ignoring the directions I don't get far

I grew up in the big city
But local politics are always in my view
You pour yourself twelve ounces
But you never drink more than two

I'm a different type of Dad than you grew up with
But I love our kids just the same
Not much in common with my mother
Dedication with a different name

Your idiosyncrasies make you my Dolly
They are what make you one of a kind
Perfect for me, God's creation
His most amazing design

I've learned it's not just a saying
It has proven to be a fact
Michael and Lana were made for each other
Because opposites attract!

Happy Valentine's Day 2015
Love,
Michael

Valentine's Day 2016

MY DAILY DEVOTIONAL

I'm not sure of the answer
Life has me confused
One minute I'm on top of the world
The next minute I feel bruised

If I were the architect
I would have used a different design
I would hand out only blessings
Challenges would be left unassigned

Some mornings I find it a challenge
To hit the ground running
Your eagerness to get things started
I find truly stunning

While I stay behind
And in the bed I still lay
You're already planning to encourage
One person that day

I worry about the problems
Which lay ahead of me concealed
I hear you speaking life
"I'm Happy, I'm Healthy, I'm Healed"

How does the person
In the center of a storm
Become everyone's cheerleader
This isn't the norm

Watching you fight
Makes me emotional
Seeing how you live your life
Is my daily devotional

It's an honor to be your husband
And for the 22nd time
Tell you I love you
In the form of a rhyme

Happy Valentine's Day 2016
I Love You,
Michael

Valentine's Day 2017

UNCHARTED

Every year at this time
I stare at a blank piece of paper
Searching for the right words
One by one they disappear like vapor

I shut myself off from the world
As it's always a struggle to get started
Until I finally remember
All great journeys begin uncharted

Of course I would prefer
The certainties of a map
Knowing where the best footholds were
I could avoid every trap

Now twenty-three years later
The night you asked me to Dance
Do you remember how nervous you were
Right before you took that chance

Or when we decided to have children
Before each birth I nearly froze
Worried they would be healthy
Until I could count 10 fingers and 10 toes

When you found our first house
And I learned it was so far away
How was I going to make a living
Weren't we safer living halfway

Living in three month increments
And anticipating the next scan
Recognizing that not knowing
Is actually part of God's plan

Then watching you receive bad news
And then seeing the doctors face
When you tell him you're going to be fine
Because you're living in God's grace

They may say I'm the writer
This might be true
But I wouldn't have anything to write about
If I didn't have you!

You in turn are the fighter
Exemplifying style and grace
You jump out of airplanes
With a smile on your face

What do you call something you've been given
Not earned and lights up your life
Most people call that a blessing
I simply call her my wife!

Happy Valentine's Day 2017,
Michael

Valentine's Day 2018

QUEEN

Is this year any different
Than the ones we have shared in the past
Time seems to be racing by
Is this year better than the last

Am I still the selfish boy
That found you at the Dance
Have I improved at all
Have I made any advance

When I think of our kids
During the moments I am most proud
They are usually exhibiting qualities
From you they were endowed

When I look at the beauty
That surrounds us at home
The vivid colors your spirit paints
Makes mine seem monochrome

The secret to a great painting
Is in the painters hand
The key to great music
Is the musicianship of the band

A delicious meal is possible
When the right ingredients are found
But the success of the people is determined
If the right Queen is crowned

And that's what you are to me
My consort for life
And my best friend too
Not merely my wife

You set our course
We pretend I'm at the wheel
Allowing me to think I'm in charge
Has always been part of the deal

You are more exquisite each day
My life's crown jewel
You're needed more than ever
I'm honored to be under your rule

Love,
Michael

Wedding Day in Kauai
04/17/97

Our first child
Age 2
Cole Francis Carouba

Big brother loving our 2nd child
Mia Grace Carouba

Mia age 2

Our kids on our first family vacation to Hawaii

A family photo taken at the park

Young Parents

Our family likes Hawaii!

Family photo in the vineyards

Lana's 50th birthday
Skydiving

Cole playing football at Lodi High

Mia play's Varsity tennis at Lodi High

Prom Night

Cole's senior picture

Having a great time in Mexico

Mia selected to the Homecoming Court

Cole off to college

Playa Del Carmen
2017

Lana in infusion at UCSF

Miracles happen!

Printed in the United States
By Bookmasters